FAMILY LIFE
HOMEBU...
COUPLES SERIES

D0345701

MASTERING MONEY IN YOUR MARRIAGE

RON BLUE

DENNIS RAINEY, SENIOR EDITOR

PERSONAL STUDY GUIDE

"UNLESS THE LORD BUILDS THE HOUSE
THEY LABOR IN VAIN WHO BUILD IT."
Psalm 127:1

Gospel Light

How to
Let the Lord
Build Your House
and not labor in vain

FamilyLife is a part of Campus Crusade for Christ International, an evangelical Christian organization founded in 1951 by Bill Bright. FamilyLife was started in 1976 to help fulfill the Great Commission by strengthening marriages and families and then equipping them to go to the world with the gospel of Jesus Christ. Our FamilyLife Marriage Conference, known as "A Weekend to Remember," is held in most major cities throughout the United States and is one of the fastest-growing marriage conferences in America today. Information on all resources offered by FamilyLife may be obtained by either writing or calling us at the address and telephone number listed below.

■

The HomeBuilders Couples Series: A small-group Bible study dedicated to making your family all that God intended.

Mastering Money In Your Marriage—Study Guide
ISBN 0-8307-1624-6

Dennis Rainey, Director
FamilyLife
P.O. Box 23840
Little Rock, AR 72221-3840
(501) 223-8663

A Ministry of Campus Crusade for Christ International
Bill Bright, Founder and President

Published by Gospel Light, Ventura, California 93006

CONTENTS

ACKNOWLEDGMENTS

There are many to whom I am deeply indebted for encouragement, assistance, and critical evaluation in the production of this Bible study. Dennis Rainey approached me in 1988 with the prospect of preparing this study and saw something in what I had done that I did not see. He was confident that the materials I had developed in ministering to others could be used in a much more significant way and minister to far greater numbers of people. I am thankful to Dennis and his wife, Barbara, for modeling many things for me and, most of all, for modeling a marriage and family.

Dave Boehi has been a very sensitive, gentle, but effective editor through this process. He has encouraged me through many revisions without being critical in any way. He has been extremely encouraging, and I sincerely appreciated the time spent working with him.

I am also very appreciative of Julie Denker's work from the beginning of the project. What she did in editing and in coordinating the field test was largely unseen, but very valuable and meaningful to me.

On any writing project that I do, I must acknowledge the contribution of my family and staff. My wife and children have been patient and helpful throughout the whole process. My staff also has suffered through changes in schedule that never seemed to end.

Last of all, I appreciate the comments and constructive criticism which came from the test groups who have contributed a great deal to making this study whatever it is.

How to
Let the Lord
Build Your House

FOREWORD

When it came time to select an author for the subject of finances in The HomeBuilders Couples Series, several fine names came to mind. And after careful consideration, we determined that there is nobody more qualified to design a practical, small-group Bible study for you than Ron Blue.

Not only is Ron a best-selling author, a Christian leader, a director of a large organization, and a board member of some excellent Christian organizations, but he is a dedicated family man as well. Ron and his wife, Judy, are committed to helping others manage their money well, and they want their five children to learn the same principles.

Wrapped in these pages of *Mastering Money in Your Marriage* are challenging questions which will lead you and your mate to evaluate the kind of stewards you are of that which God has entrusted to you. It will spark the contemplation and ignite the interaction that you need to bring about change in how you handle your checkbook.

Ron delivers what you and I need in a culture of tremendous pressure and change. You will have the opportunity to interact with your mate and with other couples over the questions found in this study. Then, at the end of each session, you'll find some "blue chip" projects that will enable you to move the convictions you develop from this study into practical application and day-to-day living.

This study is solidly biblical and simply practical. You will find, as my wife, Barbara, and I have, that Ron Blue will equip you and your mate to work through difficulties in the financial area and come up with a sound financial plan. You are going to like this study so much that you will probably find yourself wanting to go through it again in a couple of years!

DENNIS RAINEY
Director of FamilyLife

The HomeBuilders

C O U P L E S S E R I E S

"Unless the Lord builds the house,
they labor in vain who build it."
Psalm 127:1

What Is The HomeBuilders Couples Series?

Do you remember the first time you fell in love? That junior high—or elementary school—crush stirred your affections with little or no effort on your part. We use the term "falling in love" to describe the phenomenon of suddenly discovering our emotions have been captured by someone delightful.

Unfortunately, our society tends to make us think that all loving relationships should be equally as effortless. Thus, millions of couples, Christians included, approach their marriages certain that their emotions will carry them through any difficulties. And millions of couples quickly learn that a good marriage does not automatically happen.

Otherwise intelligent people, who would not think of buying a car, investing money, or even going to the grocery store without some initial planning, enter into marriage with no plan of how to make their marriages succeed.

But God has already provided the plan, a set of blueprints for a truly godly marriage. His plan is designed to enable two people to grow together in a mutually satisfying relationship, and then to look beyond their own marriage to others. Ignoring this plan leads to isolation and separation between husband and wife, the pattern so evident in the majority of homes today. Even when great energy is expended, failure to follow God's blueprints results in wasted effort, bitter disappointment—and, in far too many cases, divorce.

In response to this need in marriages today, FamilyLife of Campus Crusade for Christ is developing a series of small-group

How Do You Build a Distinctively Christian Marriage?

9

It is our hope that in answering this question with the biblical blueprints for building a home, we will see the development of growing, thriving marriages filled with the love of Jesus Christ.

FamilyLife of Campus Crusade for Christ is committed to strengthening your family. We hope The HomeBuilders Couples Series will assist you and your church as it equips couples in building godly homes.

This study, *Mastering Money in Your Marriage*, is designed to provide information about finances from a biblical perspective and show how you as a couple can master that area in your marriage. It is composed of seven sessions, each built around a concept which will enrich your marriage in the following weeks.

The Bible: Your Blueprints for a Godly Marriage

> The Bible is alive, it speaks to me;
> it has feet, it runs after me;
> it has hands, it lays hold on me.
>
> Martin Luther

You will notice as you proceed through this study that the Bible is referred to frequently as the final authority on the issues of life and marriage. Although written centuries ago, this Book still speaks clearly and powerfully about the conflicts and struggles faced by men and women. The Bible is God's Word and contains His blueprints for building a godly home and for dealing with the practical issues of living.

While Scripture has only one primary interpretation, there may be several appropriate applications. Some of the passages used in this series were not originally written with marriage in mind, but they can be applied practically to the husband-wife relationship.

We encourage you to have a Bible with you for each session. The *New King James Version*, the *New American Standard Bible*, and the *New International Version* are three excellent English translations which make the Bible easy to understand.

Ground Rules for These Sessions

These sessions are designed to be enjoyable and informative—and nonthreatening. Three simple ground rules will help ensure that everyone feels comfortable and gets the most out of the study:

1. Share nothing about your marriage that will embarrass your mate.

2. You may "pass" on any question you do not want to answer.

3. Each time between sessions, complete the **HomeBuilders Project** (questions for each couple to discuss and act on). Share one result at the next group meeting.

Resources

FamilyLife recommends these outstanding aids to maximize your HomeBuilders study experience.

1. If you are doing this as a couple, we would recommend one Study Guide for each spouse. The Leader's Guide would also be very beneficial.

2. By purchasing Ron Blue's book, *Master Your Money* (Nashville: Thomas Nelson, 1986), you can enhance the maximum effect of this study on your lives.

3. If you have attended the FamilyLife Marriage Conference, you will find the conference manual to be a useful tool as you go through The HomeBuilders Couples Series.

4. Your best resource is one another—others can help us maximize our lives as we learn to be accountable for our actions and lives. Be accountable to one another and to another couple for the session and projects completion.

HOMEBUILDERS PRINCIPLES

HomeBuilders Principle #1: No amount of wealth will ever satisfy a person's basic needs for security and significance, which can only be met by God.

HomeBuilders Principle #2: God owns it all.

HomeBuilders Principle #3: God uses money to help you mature in your faith.

HomeBuilders Principle #4: Stewardship means using the resources God has entrusted to you to accomplish His plans and purposes.

HomeBuilders Principle #5: Money is not an end in itself. It's a tool which you can use to meet God's priorities.

HomeBuilders Principle #6: Husbands and wives will have different financial priorities reflecting their differing priorities of life.

HomeBuilders Principle #7: There is no such thing as an independent financial decision. Each decision you make will influence every future financial decision.

HomeBuilders Principle #8: Delayed gratification means giving up today's desires in order to meet future needs or desires.

HomeBuilders Principle #9: A faith goal is a measurable and attainable objective toward which I believe God wants me to move.

HomeBuilders Principle #10: Debt is never the real problem, but is only symptomatic of the real problem—such as greed, self-indulgence, impatience, or lack of self-discipline.

HomeBuilders Principle #11: Borrowing money with no sure way to repay always presumes upon the future.

HomeBuilders Principle #12: Borrowing money is not a sin, but not repaying a debt is.

HomeBuilders Principle #13: Borrowing money may deny God an opportunity to show Himself faithful.

HomeBuilders Principle #14: Giving is returning to God what He already owns.

HomeBuilders Principle #15: Giving is a result of spiritual growth, not a cause of spiritual growth.

HomeBuilders Principle #16: Your children will learn more about managing money from your example than from your words.

HomeBuilders Principle #17: The greatest legacy you can leave to children is wisdom.

A WORD ABOUT
FINANCES

Did you know that the Bible contains over 2,000 verses dealing with money and money management? I think this reflects God's understanding of human nature, and the fact that how people handle their money reveals much about their character and spiritual commitment.

Any married couple will attest to the fact that many of their conflicts and disagreements revolve around their finances. So this study has two primary objectives in mind for you: (1) to help you identify and grapple with some of the biblical principles and issues regarding the whole concept of wealth and money management, and (2) to provide you with some practical guidance for handling your own personal finances.

You'll find that *Mastering Money in Your Marriage* is as much a financial workbook as it is a small-group Bible study. The exercises you'll go through—determining your net worth, budgeting, etc.—are crucial if you want to be serious about handling your money wisely. Many people hear these biblical principles but don't act on them; my prayer is that you'll take the time to *apply* what you'll learn.

RON BLUE

The HomeBuilders

C O U P L E S   S E R I E S

"Unless the Lord builds the house,
they labor in vain who build it."
Psalm 127:1

Focus

*Managing money wisely
is a challenge for any couple,
regardless of income level.*

1. Introduce yourself to the group by sharing the following information:

■ name,

■ number of children (if any),

■ occupation,

■ how long you've been married,

■ one expectation you have in joining this study.

Use the space below to record your new knowledge of the others in your group.

_____

_____

_____

_____

_____

_____

2. Share with the group the most outrageous promise that you saw or heard in an advertisement this week.

3. What does our culture communicate through advertising about money and possessions? Record the comments of the group below.

_____

_____

_____

_____

We live in a world which worships money but doesn't know how to use it wisely. The world says, Spend! Spend! Spend! Unfortunately it also says, Borrow! Borrow! Borrow! As a result, many institutions—including the American government—and many individuals find it all too easy to get into financial trouble.

A. The Need for a Plan

1. What are some of the common financial questions and struggles faced by all couples? By *Christian* couples?

_____

_____

_____

2. How do most couples respond to these struggles?

_____

_____

3. How do you currently go about making good financial decisions?

_____

_____

4. How do you think a Christian ought to live in our culture, materially speaking? What's an appropriate lifestyle?

_____

_____

5. Try the following game. When the leader says go, you have 30 seconds to find the number 1, circle it, find the number 2, circle it, and so on, until you have circled all 90 numbers. Do not start until the leader says go. You must find the numbers in sequence.

```
1          61          13          42          74          14
    41          9              70
        45          81      18          22      46
17          21              86
    89          49              34      2      30
  37    5       69      38                  50
      85              78      6          10
        29                  90
25              65      82          26          58
      33              54          62
  53          57          66
      73          77
    15      79    39          32          76      16
31                  71
      3          55          80          8      40
                      28      24      56
47      83              72          52
              27                          4
    7          67          12
      51          11              88
75                                      60
          36          20
    19      23      43          48
      87              44
35              59    63      68          84      64
```

a. What feelings did you experience as you looked for numbers?

_____

_____

b. What is the key to completing the task quickly?

_____

_____

c. How does this exercise depict the challenge of managing money wisely?

_____

_____

This game shows how most people approach their finances. There are always more alternative ways to spend money than money available, and approaching these alternatives without a plan—as many people do—usually results in frustration and confusion. Having a plan helps you sort through the alternatives to meet your own unique financial needs.

(to be completed as a couple)

Answer the following questions:

$1.$ What are one or two of your family's *current* or *long-term* financial needs?

_____

_____

_____

$2.$ What do you believe your top two highest financial priorities should be?

_____

_____

3. Conclude your time together by reading the following personal pledge statement:

"**I pledge to you that I will use the next six weeks of this HomeBuilders study to build, strengthen, and encourage our marriage. I will make this study a priority in my schedule by faithfully keeping our 'dates,' working through the projects, and participating in the group discussions. You have my word on it.**"

_____   _____

(signed)   **(date)**

Will you honor your mate by making this pledge your special commitment to him or her for the coming weeks? If so, sign your name in the space provided in *your mate's* Study Guide to document your commitment.

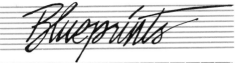

B. How Do We Meet Our Needs?

1. Read Luke 16:19–31.

a. How *secure* did the rich man believe he was when he was alive? From God's perspective, did his riches have any bearing on how God viewed him?

_____

_____

b. How *significant* was the rich man to other people? To God?

_____

_____

2. How do couples attempt to meet their need for *security* with money?

_____

_____

3. How do couples attempt to meet their need for *significance* with money?

_____

_____

4. Read Philippians 4:19. Where should your security and significance come from?

_____

_____

> **HomeBuilders Principle #1: No amount of wealth will ever satisfy a person's basic needs for security and significance, which can only be met by God.**

5. What is the most important insight you have gained in this session?

_____

_____

Each of the seven sessions in this study will end with a **Make a Date**. This is the time you set outside each session to do the **HomeBuilders Projects** you'll find at the end of each session. This will be your *only* homework. Do not begin working on the next session until you meet together again as a group. Do only the assigned **HomeBuilders Project** between sessions.

Now conclude Session One by setting aside at least one hour in this week's schedule to complete **HomeBuilders Project #1.** This project may take some time to complete, but it will help you begin to develop your own financial plan together. Your leaders will ask you at the next session to share one thing from this experience.

Date	Time	Location

■

Master Your Money   by Ron Blue

■   "Will I Ever Have Enough?" is the subject covered in chapter 1, pp. 11–16, in *Master Your Money.* This will help you consider further the issues discussed in this session.

■   Before your next session you may want to read chapter 7, pp. 69–98, in *Master Your Money.* This chapter deals with the issue of "Where Am I?"

The one financial statement which summarizes every financial transaction that a couple has ever made is the *net worth statement.* A net worth statement is a picture at a particular point in time of the true financial position of a family—a listing of the assets they own and the total debts or liabilities they owe. Subtracting the liabilities from the assets gives the net worth. If you measure your net worth periodically, you'll be able to see whether or not you are making progress toward your financial goals.

In general, *assets owned* tend to give one financial security, whereas *liabilities* or *debts owed* subtract from security. The net worth, then, could be stated as a family's net financial security.

Whether or not the assets owned are liquid (quickly convertible to cash) or nonliquid can also have an impact on financial security. Generally speaking, the more liquid the assets are, the more flexibility a couple has in their financial situation.

Additionally, speaking of liabilities, the shorter the debt term, the less secure the financial position. The reason is that short-term debt such as installment debt or credit card debt comes due every month and has a first-priority call on a family's income.

29

Completing the following charts could take quite a bit of time, but they are crucial to the remainder of this HomeBuilders study. You won't improve your financial situation until you gain a clear picture of where you stand.

Individually—15–20 Minutes

1. List the areas of *confidence* that you have regarding your personal financial situation.

_____

_____

_____

_____

2. List your greatest *concerns* regarding your personal financial situation.

_____

_____

_____

Interact As a Couple

1. Discuss your answers to the previous two questions.

2. Using the charts on the next few pages, list your assets and liabilities and determine your net worth.

ASSETS

LIQUID: (convertible into cash within seven days)
Cash on hand and checking account balance $_____

Money market funds   _____

CDs (interest rate _____%)   _____

Savings (interest rate _____%)   _____

Marketable securities   _____

Life insurance cash values   _____

_____   _____

        TOTAL LIQUID ASSETS $_____
        (Transfer the total to the
        personal balance sheet analysis.)

NONLIQUID (cannot be sold quickly except at a loss)
Home (market value) $_____

Land (market value)   _____

Business valuation   _____

Real estate investments   _____

Limited partnerships   _____

Boat, camper, tractor, etc.   _____

Automobile(s) (market value)   _____

Furniture and personal property
(estimated market value)   _____

Coin and stamp collections, antiques   _____

IRAs, Keogh   _____

Pension and profit sharing   _____

Receivables from others   _____

_____   _____

        TOTAL NONLIQUID ASSETS $_____
        (Transfer the total to the
        personal balance sheet analysis.)

LIABILITIES

	CREDITOR	INTEREST RATE	BALANCE DUE
1.	_____	_____	$_____
2.	_____	_____	_____
3.	_____	_____	_____
4.	_____	_____	_____
5.	_____	_____	_____
6.	_____	_____	_____
7.	_____	_____	_____
8.	_____	_____	_____
9.	_____	_____	_____
10.	_____	_____	_____

TOTAL LIABILITIES $ _____
(Transfer the total to the
personal balance sheet analysis.)

PERSONAL BALANCE SHEET ANALYSIS

(Date: _____)

Liquid assets $_____

Plus nonliquid assets   + _____

TOTAL ASSETS   = _____

Less TOTAL LIABILITIES   − _____

NET WORTH   = _____

The HomeBuilders

C O U P L E S   S E R I E S

"Unless the Lord builds the house,
they labor in vain who build it."
Psalm 127:1

Stewardship is the management of
God's resources for the
accomplishment of God-given goals.

1. Begin this session by sharing one thing you learned from **HomeBuilders Project #1**.

2. Let's say that last week you loaned your brand-new car to a friend. When he returned the car, it had a crumpled fender, broken headlight, and missing bumper. When he handed you the keys, he said he was sorry for all the damage and wondered if you would mind loaning him the car again this week. He also asked if you could have all the repairs completed before he borrowed the car again.

How would you feel if this happened to you?

_____

_____

3. What would you say to your friend?

_____

_____

4.   Why should you expect a friend to treat your property differently than this one did?

_____

_____

In this study we are going to explore how our stewardship of God's property is an important measure of our faithfulness to Him.

A. What's Your Attitude?

1. From what you've observed, what guidelines do most people use in managing their money?

_____

_____

2. How should the couple which uses the Bible as a guide manage their money differently than the couple which does not?

_____

_____

3. Have any of your previous attitudes about money changed because of a new biblical perspective? Which ones?

_____

_____

B. Illustration of a Steward

Webster's Dictionary defines a *steward* as "one who acts as a supervisor or administrator, as of finances and property, for another or others." The Bible makes it clear that God sees us as stewards of the financial resources He entrusts to us.

Read Genesis 39:1–6, 21–23

1. How much did Joseph own? _____

2. Why didn't the owners concern themselves with what they had entrusted to Joseph?

_____

_____

3. How can this apply to you?

_____

_____

(to be completed as a couple)

1. Individually, list below your five most important material possessions—those you would most hate to lose (don't include "family" in this list).

_____

_____

_____

_____

_____

2. With your mate, discuss your reasons for choosing each item on your list.

C. Three Biblical Principles of Money Management

1. Read Psalm 24:1. How should the fact expressed in this verse affect the way you handle your finances?

_____

_____

HomeBuilders Principle #2: God owns it all.

---

2. Read Matthew 25:14–30. What were the responsibilities of the servants in this parable?

_____

_____

3. What rewards did the servants receive?

_____

_____

4. How has God used money to help you grow in your faith?

_____

_____

> **HomeBuilders Principle #3: God uses money to help you mature in your faith.**

5. What does this parable say about your own stewardship responsibilities?

_____

_____

6. Why was the unfaithful steward called unfaithful?

_____

_____

7. According to James 2:17, what does faith require? How does this principle apply to your stewardship responsibilities?

_____

_____

8. Can you recall a time when you've used resources God has entrusted to you to accomplish His plans?

_____

_____

HomeBuilders Principle #4: **Stewardship means using the
resources God has entrusted to you to accomplish His plans
and purposes.**

D. Tests of a Steward

1. Read Luke 16:10–13. What are the three tests of a steward
listed in verses 10–12?

_____

_____

_____

2. Why is it that people can't serve both God and money? How
has this been true in your life?

_____

_____

3. What **HomeBuilders Principle** from this session do you think
you need to apply more than any other?

_____

_____

43

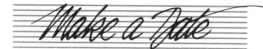

Make a date with your mate to meet in the next few days to complete **HomeBuilders Project #2.** Your leader will ask you at the next session to share one thing from this experience.

Date	Time	Location

■

Recommended Reading

Master Your Money   by Ron Blue

■ "Four Biblical Principles of Money Management" is the subject covered in chapter 2, pp. 17–24 in *Master Your Money*. This will help you consider further issues discussed in this session.

Individually—15–20 Minutes

1. Reflect on a recent frustration you've had regarding money. What do you think God is trying to teach you?

_____

_____

_____

_____

2. Review your list of most important possessions from this session's **Construction** exercise. Are there any possessions on that list over which you are now exercising ownership "rights" rather than steward-ship "responsibilities"?

_____

_____

_____

_____

3. In what ways have you struggled over acknowledging God's total ownership of your resources?

_____

_____

Interact As a Couple—20–35 Minutes

1. Discuss your answers to the previous two questions.

2. Consider how you can help each other maintain the perspective that God owns everything.

3. Together in prayer commit to give back to the true Owner His resources and to take up your stewardship responsibility.

4. In biblical days a covenant meant much the same thing that a contract does today. On the next page, write out your own covenant—with each other and with God—declaring that God is the Owner of everything you have and that He has placed you as stewards of those resources.

Remember to bring your calendar for **Make a Date** to your next session. Also, bring your checkbook to the next session; it will be useful for an important learning exercise.

OUR FINANCIAL COVENANT

_____

_____

_____

_____

_____

_____

_____

_____

_____

_____

_____

_____

_____

_____

_____

_____

_____

_____	_____
(signed)	(date)

_____	_____
(signed)	(date)

The HomeBuilders

COUPLES SERIES

"Unless the Lord builds the house,
they labor in vain who build it."
Psalm 127:1

Focus

Every financial decision you make is
ultimately a priority decision.

1. Share with the group one thing you learned from **HomeBuilders Project #2**.

2. You have just been notified that your Great Aunt Harriet passed away at age 100. In her will she designated $50,000 in cash for you to use as you would like, *but it all must be designated or spent within 30 days*.

List below how you would spend the money.

Item _____

Cost $_____

Item _____

Cost $_____

Item _____

Cost $_____

Item _____

Cost $_____

Item _____

Cost $_____

Item _____

Cost $_____

3. Share with the group what you put on your list and why.

A. The Source of Financial Priorities

1. Look at your checkbook (or, if you don't have it with you, think about the checks you've written over the last month). What conclusions can you reach from this evidence about your priorities in spending money?

_____

_____

2. Would you say that your current financial priorities are long-term or short-term?

_____

_____

3. How would you say the world influences you as you set financial priorities?

_____

_____

4. How does God influence your financial priorities?

_____

_____

5. What are some nonfinancial priorities God has given you?

_____

_____

6. How can you use money to help you meet these priorities?

_____

_____

HomeBuilders Principle #5: Money is not an end in itself. It's a tool which you can use to meet God's priorities.

(to be completed as a couple)

1. Discuss with your spouse the lists developed in Question 1 in the **Warm Up**.

2. See how quickly you can agree on a joint list. There must be 100 percent agreement, and there must be at least three items on the list.

Item _____

Cost $_____

Item _____

Cost $_____

Item _____

Cost $_____

Item _____

Cost $_____

Item _____

Cost $_____

Item _____

Cost $_____

B. Conflict over Financial Priorities

1. Discuss with the group how you and your mate arrived at your decision from the **Construction** project.

2. What are some of the ways couples in the group differ in how they make decisions?

_____

_____

_____

_____

3. How do you and your mate resolve disagreements involving finances?

_____

_____

_____

_____

4. What do you think is the true cause of your disagreements?

_____

_____

5. Disagreement over financial decisions is inevitable between any two people because each will have different priorities for spending the money. In what ways do your priorities differ from your mate's?

_____

_____

_____

_____

HomeBuilders Principle #6: Husbands and wives will have different financial priorities reflecting their differing priorities of life.

One way for couples to avoid conflict over money decisions is to agree on their priorities as a couple, recognizing legitimate differences and the need for individual give and take. Examining the biblical priorities for using money can aid a couple in developing their mutual financial priorities.

C. Biblical Priorities for the Use of Money

1. The Bible includes over 2,000 verses dealing with money and money management. What do the following groups of verses say about what these priorities should be?

a. Proverbs 3:9, 10; and 1 Corinthians 16:2 _____

_____

_____

b. Psalm 37:21 _____

_____

c. Romans 13:6–7 and Matthew 22:21 _____

_____

_____

d. 1 Timothy 5:8 _____

_____

_____

e. Proverbs 6:6–11 and Proverbs 31:16 _____

_____

_____

2. How well do you think your present financial priorities line up with these biblical priorities?

_____

_____

_____

_____

BIBLICAL PRIORITIES AND THE
FINANCIAL PLANNING PROCESS

The following diagram of the financial planning process shows the crucial role biblical priorities play in financial planning. When you solidify your financial situation by appropriately dividing your income among the five priority uses of money the Bible specifies, you'll begin developing the ability to meet the long-range objectives shown at the bottom of the diagram.

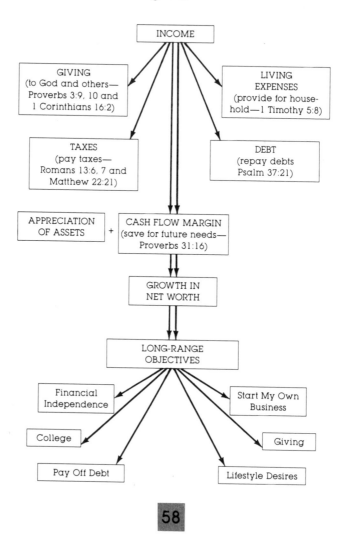

D. Interdependence of Financial Decisions

1. When you spend money to meet a short-term desire, how does that affect subsequent financial decisions?

_____

_____

> HomeBuilders Principle #7: There is no such thing as an independent financial decision. Each decision you make will influence every future financial decision.

2. What do you think you'd need to do to begin ordering your finances around the biblical priorities mentioned?

_____

_____

3. What changes would you need to make in your lifestyle?

_____

_____

> HomeBuilders Principle #8: Delayed gratification means giving up today's desires in order to meet future needs or desires.

4. Why do you think **HomeBuilders Principle #8** is especially difficult to practice while living in this culture?

_____

_____

5. How do you break the grip of the need for immediate gratification?

_____

_____

6. What principle from this session do you most want to apply in your life?

_____

_____

Make a date with your mate to meet in the next few days to complete **HomeBuilders Project #3**. Your leader will ask you at the next session to share one thing from this experience.

Date	Time	Location

■

Master Your Money   by Ron Blue

■ "A Financial Planning Overview" is the subject covered in chapter 3, pp. 25–31, in *Master Your Money*. This will help you consider further the issues discussed in this session.

■ "Guaranteed Financial Success" is the subject covered in chapter 4, pp. 32–42, in *Master Your Money*, and "Where Am I?" is the subject covered in chapter 7, pp. 69–99, in *Master Your Money*. These will help you consider further the issues discussed in this session.

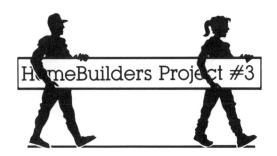

HomeBuilders Project #3

By completing the following charts, you will gain a clearer understanding of what your financial priorities have been until now. (People are often surprised to see what their actual financial priorities are—as compared to what they believe them to be.) You'll also be able to start making decisions about where to change your spending habits. Understanding where you are now spending money is the first step to getting control of your finances. This exercise will begin to give you tremendous freedom in your financial life as you take control over your spending.

$1.$ Complete the Living Expense Summary and Cash Flow Analysis on pages 64-7 either as planned this year or as it actually happened last year.

$2.$ Discuss what the analysis reveals about your actual financial priorities.

$3.$ What would you like your actual priorities to be, and how should those priorities be reflected in how you allocate your money?

	PRIORITY	AMOUNT ($) OR PERCENT (%)
1st	_____	_____
2nd	_____	_____
3rd	_____	_____
4th	_____	_____
5th	_____	_____

LIVING EXPENSES SUMMARY
(Date: _____)

	AMOUNT PAID MONTHLY	AMOUNT PAID OTHER THAN MONTHLY	TOTAL AMOUNT PAID
HOUSING			
Mortgage/rent	_____	_____	_____
Insurance	_____	_____	_____
Property taxes	_____	_____	_____
Electricity	_____	_____	_____
Heating	_____	_____	_____
Water	_____	_____	_____
Sanitation	_____	_____	_____
Telephone	_____	_____	_____
Cleaning	_____	_____	_____
Repairs/ Maintenance	_____	_____	_____
Supplies	_____	_____	_____
Other	_____	_____	_____
TOTAL	_____	_____	_____
FOOD	_____	_____	_____
CLOTHING	_____	_____	_____
TRANSPORTATION			
Insurance	_____	_____	_____
Gas and oil	_____	_____	_____
Maintenance/ Repairs	_____	_____	_____
Parking	_____	_____	_____
Other	_____	_____	_____
TOTAL	_____	_____	_____

	AMOUNT PAID MONTHLY	AMOUNT PAID OTHER THAN MONTHLY	TOTAL AMOUNT PAID
ENTERTAINMENT/RECREATION			
Eating out			
Movies, concerts, etc.			
Baby-sitters			
Magazines/ Newspapers			
Vacation			
Clubs and activities			
Other			
TOTAL			
MEDICAL EXPENSES			
Insurance			
Doctors			
Dentists			
Medication			
TOTAL			
INSURANCE (NONMEDICAL)			
Life			
Disability			
Other			
TOTAL			

	AMOUNT PAID. MONTHLY	AMOUNT PAID OTHER THAN MONTHLY	TOTAL AMOUNT PAID
CHILDREN			
School lunches	_____	_____	_____
Allowances	_____	_____	_____
Tuition	_____	_____	_____
Lessons	_____	_____	_____
Other	_____	_____	_____
TOTAL	_____	_____	_____
GIFTS			
Christmas	_____	_____	_____
Birthdays	_____	_____	_____
Anniversaries	_____	_____	_____
Other	_____	_____	_____
TOTAL	_____	_____	_____
MISCELLANEOUS			
Toiletries	_____	_____	_____
Husband misc.	_____	_____	_____
Wife misc.	_____	_____	_____
Cleaning, laundry	_____	_____	_____
Animal care	_____	_____	_____
Hair care	_____	_____	_____
Other	_____	_____	_____
Other	_____	_____	_____
TOTAL	_____	_____	_____
TOTAL LIVING EXPENSES	_____	_____	_____

CASH FLOW ANALYSIS

(Date: _____)

GROSS INCOME $_____

EXPENSES OF INCOME:
   Giving $ _____

   Taxes   + _____

   Debt   + _____

   Social Security   + _____

   Total Expenses Income   = _____   − _____

NET SPENDABLE INCOME   = _____
(Gross Income Less Expenses)

LIVING EXPENSES
   Housing $ _____

   Food   + _____

   Clothing   + _____

   Transportation   + _____

   Entertainment/Recreation   + _____

   Medical   + _____

   Insurance   + _____

   Children   + _____

   Gifts   + _____

   Miscellaneous   + _____

   Total Living Expenses   = _____   − _____

CASH FLOW MARGIN   = _____
(Net Spendable Income Less Living Expenses)

The HomeBuilders

COUPLES SERIES

"Unless the Lord builds the house,
they labor in vain who build it."
Psalm 127:1

Focus

Setting financial goals
under the guidance of the Holy Spirit
gives couples direction, motivation,
and hope.

1. Share with the group one thing you learned from **HomeBuilders Project #3.**

2. What is a goal you've set (in any area of your life) in the past, and how did the act of setting that goal help you achieve it?

_____

_____

3. If you learned today that you had five years to live, what financial goals would you set, basing your decision on the biblical priorities listed in the previous session?

_____

_____

Setting financial goals should be a key part of your financial plan. But many people don't even know what a true goal is, much less how to make goals under God's direction.

A. Why Set Goals?

1. Why don't many people set goals?

_____

_____

2. What happens to you if you don't set financial goals?

_____

_____

3. What do you think your financial situation would be like in 10 years if you set goals right now and worked to meet them?

_____

_____

B. What Is a Goal?

A goal is a measurable and attainable objective toward which I am moving. It is always future-oriented. It is always dependent upon me alone for accomplishment, and it is specific enough so that I will know when I have attained it. A goal moves me toward the accomplishment of broader purposes.

1. According to the preceding definition, which of the following are goals? (Circle the letters that apply.)

a. To be a good father or mother.

b. To be a good husband or wife.

c. To be godly.

d. To have a nice home.

e. To earn $1,000,000 per day by age 30.

f. To buy my own jet next week.

g. To spend 15 minutes with each of my children tomorrow.

h. To take my wife to dinner Friday night.

i. To have a "quiet time" five times per week.

j. To earn $75,000 per year by age 50.

k. To have a four-bedroom, three-bath home on one acre within 15 minutes of schools and the office.

2. If *a* through *d* are not goals, what are they?

_____

_____

3. Why are *e* and *f* not goals?

_____

_____

4. What are the two characteristics of *g* through *k* that make them goals?

_____

_____

(to be completed as a couple)

1. Individually, write down one goal that you set and accomplished during the last twelve months.

_____

_____

2. Share and discuss the above answer with your mate.

3. As a couple, set a measurable and attainable goal (financial or otherwise) to accomplish within the next 30 days. Be specific!

_____

_____

C. How to Set Goals Which Are God's

1. *Step One: Be filled with the Holy Spirit.*

a. What are you promised in John 14:16–18? Verse 26?

_____

_____

b. What are you commanded to do in Ephesians 5:18?

_____

_____

The Holy Spirit is the third person of the Trinity: Father, Son, and Holy Spirit. When a person by faith receives Christ, the Holy Spirit *regenerates* him (John 3:5), *baptizes* him into the Body of Christ (1 Corinthians 12:13), and *comes to dwell within* him (1 Corinthians 3:16). (Note: If you have never received Christ as your Savior, read the appendix, "The Four Spiritual Laws," at the end of this HomeBuilders study.)

The Holy Spirit will never leave you, but being filled (controlled and empowered) by the Holy Spirit is a process which will be repeated many times as you yield yourself to Christ and His authority over your life. Many Christians live defeated and unproductive lives because they have never understood how to be filled with the Spirit.

c. Read 1 John 1:9. What is the prerequisite to being filled with the Spirit?

_____

_____

d. If you confess your sins, yield your life to God, and ask Him to fill you with His Spirit, will He do it? Read Hebrews 11:6.

_____

_____

e. Why is it important to be filled with the Spirit when making financial decisions?

_____

_____

$2.$ *Step Two: Spend time with God in His Word and in prayer, asking Him what His goals are for the financial resources He has entrusted to you.*

a. What do the following verses have to say about what God will do for you as you spend time praying and reading His Word?

Psalm 119:105 _____

_____

Proverbs 3:5, 6 _____

_____

Psalm 32:8 _____

_____

b. Have you seen these verses come true in your life? If so, how?

_____

_____

3. *Step Three: Record the impressions He is making on you.*

As you spend time in the Word and in prayer, the Holy Spirit will begin to guide you in setting specific, attainable financial goals. As you write down what you sense God is telling you, be sure to ask yourself, "Does this glorify God?" or "Is this definitely biblical?" to ensure that you aren't confusing emotional desires with the Spirit's actual direction.

Can you think of a time in the past when God impressed you as a couple with a decision or goal He wanted you to make?

_____

_____

4. *Step Four: Act on the basis of faith.*

a. Read Hebrews 11:1. What is faith?

_____

_____

b. Is there a financial decision confronting you in which you need to take a faith step?

_____

_____

5. Read Nehemiah 1:1–2:8

a. What did Nehemiah do? (1:4–11 and 2:4–8)?

_____

_____

b. How then could he be so confident?

_____

_____

c. Whose goal did he really accomplish?

_____

_____

HomeBuilders Principle #9: A faith goal is a measurable and attainable objective toward which I believe God wants me to move.

SUMMARY OF THE GOAL-SETTING PROCESS

Step One: Be filled with the Holy Spirit.
Step Two: Spend time with God in His Word and in prayer, asking Him what His goals are for the financial resources He has entrusted to you.
Step Three: Record the impressions He is making on you.
Step Four: Act on the basis of faith.

Make a date with your mate to meet in the next few days to complete **HomeBuilders Project #4.** Your leader will ask you at the next session to share one thing from this experience.

Date	Time	Location

Master Your Money by Ron Blue

■ "Setting Faith Financial Goals" is the subject covered in chapter 8, pp. 99–111, in *Master Your Money*. This will help you consider further the issues discussed in this session.

The Secret by Bill Bright

■ Learn the secret of successful Christian living—walking in the power of the Holy Spirit.

Individually—15–20 Minutes

1. Review how to be filled with the Holy Spirit and take whatever steps are necessary to be personally filled.

2. Ask God in prayer what financial goals He would have you to set. Following are some areas you may want to pray about:

■ providing for your family. (This can include saving for college and helping children become financially independent.)

■ paying off debt.

■ paying taxes.

■ giving.

■ saving.

3. Record your impressions below.

_____

_____

Interact As a Couple—25-30 Minutes

1. Discuss your impressions from the time spent individually.

2. Jointly set three financial goals and list them below. (Remember that these goals must be measurable and attainable. An example would be: "Pay off all credit card debt in next 18 months.")

GOAL	$ AMOUNT	DATE TO BE ACCOMPLISHED
1.		
2.		
3.		

3. In order to begin to accomplish the goal, you must exercise faith by acting. Determine and record below the first step you will take in acting on each goal you listed above.

ACTION STEP	DATE TO BE TAKEN
1.	
2.	
3.	

Close your time together by praying for one another and for your success in meeting your financial goals.

Remember to bring your calendar to the next session for **Make a Date**.

Borrowing money usually
prevents couples from achieving
long-term financial success.

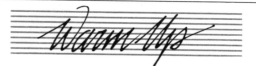

1. Begin this session by sharing one goal that you and your mate set in **HomeBuilders Project #4.**

2. Read the following vignette:

Mike was a real estate agent and his wife Jill was a nurse. Jill's mom and dad had taught her that financial responsibility is important and necessary. She learned, for example, how to save up for things she wanted rather than borrow the money. As a result, she tended to be cautious with money and reluctant to go into debt.

Mike, however, fell into the trap of impulsive buying and often found himself compelled to buy things he saw on television commercials and in magazine ads. He loved nice clothes and fancy electronic equipment, and he often purchased them on credit, thinking he'd pay for them eventually.

Mike and Jill began arguing continually about their finances, but they never found any resolution to their conflict. Eventually, they found themselves seriously in debt, behind on their house payments, and unable to pay many of their bills by the due date.

What attitudes did Mike display which caused this couple to go into debt?

_____

_____

3. What can Mike and Jill do to repair their disastrous situation?

_____

_____

4. In what ways have your attitudes about debt—good or bad—influenced you as a couple?

_____

_____

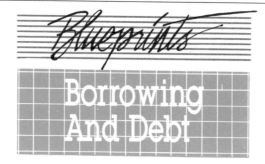

A. Some Important Definitions

Study the following basic definitions relating to issues of credit and borrowing:

■ Debt: Any money owed to anyone for anything. A financial obligation to someone.

■ Borrow: To obtain use of something belonging to someone else. (When we speak of borrowing in this chapter, we are primarily speaking of entering into a contractual obligation to pay interest in order to use someone else's money.)

■ Bankruptcy: A legal recognition of inability to repay financial obligations.

B. Why People Borrow Money

1. What are some of the reasons you give to yourself for borrowing money (whether from a lending institution or with a credit card)?

_____

_____

_____

2. Which of those, do you think, are legitimate reasons?

_____

_____

_____

HomeBuilders Principle #10. Debt is never the real problem, but is only symptomatic of the real problem—such as greed, self-indulgence, impatience, or lack of self-discipline.

C. Scriptural Insights

1. Read James 4:13, 14 and Luke 14:28–30. What biblical principles can you draw from these passages?

_____

_____

_____

2. How could borrowing money cause you to violate these principles?

_____

_____

_____

3. If you can, share how a mistake you and your mate made in misusing debt affected your life, marriage, and family during the ensuing months and years.

_____

_____

_____

_____

> **HomeBuilders Principle #11: Borrowing money with no sure way to repay always presumes upon the future.**

4. What do the following verses have to say about borrowing money?

a. Proverbs 22:7 _____

_____

b. Psalm 37:21 _____

_____

c. Proverbs 22:26, 27_____

_____

5. Do any of these verses say that borrowing money is a sin?

☐ Yes   ☐ No

6. When *is* borrowing a sin (Psalm 37:21)?

_____

_____

> HomeBuilders Principle #12: Borrowing money is not a sin, but not repaying a debt is.

(to be completed as a couple)

1. Discuss with your mate what you'd like your debt situation to be in:

a. 1 year _____

b. 5 years _____

c. 10 years _____

2. What first step can you take to accomplish the one-year goal?

_____

_____

3. List one financial decision you are making right now. Pray about that decision.

_____

_____

C. Scriptural Insights (continued)

7. Read Isaiah 55:8, 9. How does this passage relate to borrowing money?

_____

_____

8. Have you seen God work in an unusual way in your finances? Explain.

_____

_____

9. Read Philippians 4:19. How does this verse relate to money?

_____

_____

10. What is the difference between a need and a desire?

_____

_____

11. How has God provided for your needs in the past?

_____

_____

HomeBuilders Principle #13: Borrowing money may deny God an opportunity to show Himself faithful.

THE MAGIC OF COMPOUNDING

The principle of compounding has been called the eighth wonder of the world. It can either work for you or against you, depending upon whether you are a saver or a borrower. Understanding this principle will probably make you think carefully about borrowing money.

Let's say that you borrow $10,000 every four years to buy a car, and you have an average of $5,000 borrowed throughout the four-year time period. Your lender will turn around and use the interest you pay on your loan to loan more money to others.

By using the following chart, you can see how much the lender earns from your interest. For example, if you continue to finance your car purchases throughout a working life of 40 years, and the average interest rate you pay to the lender is 12 percent, by using the chart you'll find the figure 93.0. Multiply that by the average loan amount, and you'll end up with the amount of $465,000. This is the amount that the lender has earned by collecting your interest and then reloaning it to someone else at a 12-percent rate.

To state it another way, if you saved your money in an account that earned 12 percent compounded interest, you only have to make an initial deposit of $5,000 and leave it untouched for 40 years in order to have a $465,000 at the end of 40 years!

To use this chart:
(1) *Determine average bank amount.* Subtract ending balance (what you owe when you make your last payment) then divide by two.
(2) *Find number on chart* by matching interest rate and years with auto loan.
(3) *Multiply figures from (1) and (2).*

YEARS WITH AN AUTO LOAN	INTEREST RATE						
	8%	10%	12%	14%	16%	18%	21%
5	1.5	1.6	1.7	1.9	2.1	2.3	2.6
10	2.2	2.6	3.1	3.7	4.4	5.2	6.7
15	3.2	4.2	5.5	7.1	9.3	12.0	17.5
20	4.7	6.7	9.6	13.7	19.5	27.4	45.3
25	6.9	10.8	17.0	26.5	40.9	62.7	117.4
30	10.0	17.5	30.0	50.6	85.9	143.4	304.5
35	14.8	28.1	52.7	98.1	180.3	328.0	789.8
40	21.7	45.3	93.0	188.9	378.7	750.4	1048.4

Make a date with your mate to meet in the next few days to complete **HomeBuilders Project #5.** Your leader will ask you at the next session to share one thing from this experience.

Date	Time	Location

The Debt Squeeze   by Ron Blue

■ Practical guidance for getting out of debt—and avoiding it in the future.

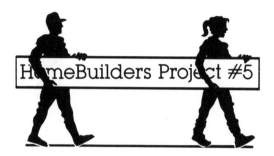

Individually—15–20 Minutes

Work through the following examination of some rules to follow in deciding whether or not to borrow money.

1. *Rule One: Borrowing needs to be in accordance with God's will.*

a. Read Colossians 3:15. What do you experience when you are following God's will?

_____

_____

b. Can you think of a time when you borrowed money without experiencing God's peace? What happened as a result?

_____

_____

2. *Rule Two: Borrowing needs to make economic sense.*

A general guideline to follow is that *the growth in value or economic return should be greater than the interest cost.* Which of the following forms of borrowing may not meet this guideline?

	MAY MEET IT	ABSOLUTELY DOES NOT MEET IT
Credit card	☐	☐
Consumer debt	☐	☐
Mortgage debt	☐	☐
Investment debt	☐	☐
Business debt	☐	☐

3. *Rule Three: There needs to be a guaranteed way to repay the loan.*

4. *Rule Four: You should be unified with your mate in the decision.*

a. Read Psalm 133:1. How should this apply to making joint decisions on borrowing money?

_____

_____

b. What should you do if you and your mate disagree on a decision?

_____

_____

Interact As a Couple—25–30 Minutes

1. Discuss together the four rules for deciding whether to borrow money that you considered individually.

97

2. Are there any decisions you are making right now about borrowing money? With the previous rules in mind, what do you think you should do?

3. If you consistently spend more than you earn and fund this deficit spending with increasing debt, you need to do two things to get out of debt. In many cases the first practical step is to decrease your spending, because that's easier than the second step, which is increasing your income.

a. Decreasing your spending in order to begin reducing your debt may mean changing your lifestyle. What are some of the *nonfinancial* costs of making this decision?

_____

_____

b. Where does the power come from to make this decision and then live with the consequences?

_____

_____

c. Using the Debt Summary chart, prepare a complete summary of all money you owe, listing lenders, amount owed, the date the loan will be paid off, and the payment schedule that has been arranged.

d. Pray together over this debt list.

e. If appropriate, set up a plan of repayment.

f. If you're ready, commit to no more borrowing unless you are in complete agreement as a couple. Sign the following pledge in *your mate's* study guide.

> "I commit to you to borrow no more money nor use credit cards as a short-term loan without your complete and freely given agreement."
>
> _____   _____
> (signed)   (date)

Close your time together by praying for one another. Remember to bring your calendar for **Make a Date** to the next session.

DEBT SUMMARY

LENDER	AMOUNT OWED	DUE DATE	PAYMENT SCHEDULE

Focus

The key to financial freedom
is giving.

1. Share with the group one principle or lesson that you learned from the last session.

2. Most of us have heard that it is "more blessed to give than to receive." Do you really think this is true? Why?

_____

_____

3. What is the most meaningful gift you've ever given, and how did God use that gift?

_____

_____

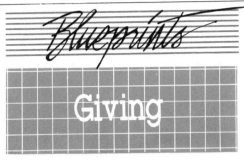

Giving

A couple's pattern of giving is one of the most effective barometers for gauging both economic and spiritual health. In this study you'll learn some biblical attitudes and guidelines that will help you in your giving decisions.

A. The Basis for Giving

1. What are some wrong motives people have for giving? What are some *right* motives?

_____

_____

2. Read Psalm 24:1, 2. Why are we sometimes reluctant to return to God what He already owns?

_____

_____

3. What do you think would happen if half the Christians in your church began giving 10 percent of their income to the Lord's work?

_____

_____

_____

> **HomeBuilders Principle #14: Giving is returning to God what He already owns.**

4. Read Matthew 6:19–21.

a. According to this scripture, what happens to your earthly treasures?

_____

_____

b. How secure are heavenly treasures?

_____

_____

c. What does verse 21 mean?

_____

_____

_____

d. Does giving *cause* a heart attitude, or is it a *result* of a heart attitude?

_____

> **HomeBuilders Principle #15: Giving is a result of spiritual growth, not a cause of spiritual growth.**

B. Principles of Giving

1.
According to Proverbs 3:9, 10, what should the priority for giving be?

_____

_____

2.
What do the following passages tell us about what or whom we should give to?

a. 1 Corinthians 16:1

_____

_____

b. Galatians 2:10

_____

_____

c. James 1:27

_____

_____

3. The Bible has much to say about what we are doing on a day-to-day basis that contributes to reaching a lost world. Sometimes we carry out these ministry activities personally; other times we do them through organizations. God has entrusted wealth to Christians so that they might use that wealth to fund biblical ministry activities. Read Matthew 28:18–20 and Acts 1:8. If these commandments reflect God's priorities, what type of ministries should you give to?

_____

_____

4. If appropriate, share a type of ministry to which you personally feel God wants you to contribute.

_____

_____

(to be completed as a couple)

1. In order to determine how you are doing in meeting the biblical priorities with your giving, check the boxes that represent areas where your giving dollars are now going.

TYPE OF MINISTRY   PLACE OF MINISTRY (ACTS 1:8)

	JERUSALEM (CITY)	JUDEA (STATE)	SAMARIA (NATION)	WORLD (WORLD)
Evangelism (Matthew 28:18–20)				
Discipleship (Matthew 28:18–20)				
Needs of Other Believers (1 Corinthians 16:1)				
Widows and Orphans (James 1:27)				
The Poor (Galatians 2:10)				

2. Discuss together what areas you'd like to begin giving to (or increase your giving to) in the future. (Caution: Be aware you can't give to everything. Ultimately, you should give to the areas you personally have a burden for.)

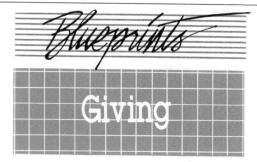

C. Attitude in Giving

1. Read 2 Corinthians 8:3, 4.

a. How did the Macedonians give?

_____

_____

b. What sacrifices would you need to make in your lifestyle in order to give in the same spirit? What things would you have to give up?

_____

_____

2. Read 2 Corinthians 8:7–9.

a. What did Jesus Christ give up?

_____

_____

b. In verse 7, giving is called _____ .

c. What does that mean?

_____

_____

3. Read Acts 4:36, 37.

a. What did Barnabas give?

_____

_____

b. How does that action reflect the meaning of his name (Son of Encouragement)?

_____

_____

4. Read 2 Corinthians 9:6, 7. In light of the three scriptural examples we have just looked at, what attitude should be evident in our giving?

_____

_____

5. The **Focus** of this session states, "The key to financial freedom is giving." How is this true?

_____

_____

_____

6. Share a time when you have experienced this truth.

_____

_____

_____

_____

7. What is the most important concept you've learned during this session?

_____

_____

_____

_____

$\mathbb{M}$ake a date with your mate to meet in the next few days to complete **HomeBuilders Project #6.** Your leader will ask you at the next session to share one thing from this experience.

Date	Time	Location

■

Master Your Money   by Ron Blue

■ "Tax Planning" is the subject covered in chapter 12, pp. 157–176, in *Master Your Money.* This will help you consider further the issues discussed in this session.

1. Review either your federal income tax returns for the last three years or last year's canceled checks and calculate what percent of your total income you gave away.

_____

2. As a couple, prayerfully set a goal for giving.

HOW MUCH	TO WHOM	WHEN
$ _____	_____	_____
$ _____	_____	_____
$ _____	_____	_____
$ _____	_____	_____
$ _____	_____	_____
$ _____	_____	_____

$3.$ What would you have to sacrifice in order to reach this giving goal?

_____

_____

Optional Activity

As a family, visit a local Christian ministry that you're interested in and determine:

■ what its financial needs are.

■ how well it uses its financial resources.

■ what the results of its ministry have been.

■ what the objectives of its ministry are.

Remember to bring your calendar for **Make a Date** to your next session.

The HomeBuilders

C O U P L E S   S E R I E S

"Unless the Lord builds the house,
they labor in vain who build it."
Psalm 127:1

Focus

Training others — especially your children and grandchildren — to manage money allows you to make an incalculable impact on future generations.

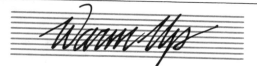

1. Share with the group one lesson or principle that you learned from the last session.

2. How do you think your children will handle money when they are on their own?

_____

_____

3. What would you like for your children to remember about the way you handle money as they begin to accept responsibility for their own financial decisions?

_____

_____

4. What would you like for them to *forget?*

_____

_____

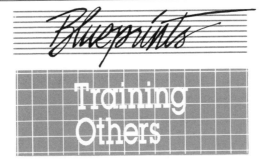

Many people handle finances poorly because no one taught them how to do it correctly. You may have a plan for your child's education and physical development, but have you developed a *financial* education plan?

Some of you may have already raised your children (or never had any children), but chances are that you could teach these principles to someone else—your grandchildren, or perhaps an employee who is falling into debt.

A. Leading By Example

1. What do you remember about the way your parents handled money?

_____

_____

2. Which do you remember more: the things your parents *taught* you about finances or the things they *showed* you through their example?

_____

Can you recall a specific story? What happened?

_____

_____

_____

_____

3. In what ways are you similar to your parents in how you handle money? Different?

_____

_____

4. What principles or techniques have you carried forward in teaching your children about finances?

_____

_____

HomeBuilders Principle #16: Your children will learn more about managing money from your example than from your words.

Construction

(to be completed as a couple)

1. Discuss the following questions.

a. Do you have a will?   ☐ Yes   ☐ No

(If you checked no, use this time to make plans for getting a will made.)

b. Where is your will located? _____

c. When was your will last reviewed by either of you or an attorney?

_____

d. Who does the will appoint as:

■ guardian(s) of your children? _____

■ executor? _____

■ trustee of your assets? _____

2. What do you think is the most important character quality to build into your children in the handling of money?

_____

_____

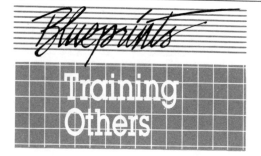

B. A Legacy for the Next Generation

1. From the **Construction** section, share the character quality you decided was most important to build into your children.

2. Read Proverbs 16:16. Why is wisdom so valuable?

_____

_____

3. How is wisdom taught?

a. Proverbs 6:20–23 _____

_____

b. Proverbs 24:30–34 _____

_____

4. Read Proverbs 22:6. What are the long-term results of teaching children wisdom?

_____

_____

5. How will gaining wisdom affect the way they handle money?

_____

_____

> **HomeBuilders Principle #17: The greatest legacy you can leave to children is wisdom.**

6. How have you taught wisdom to your kids? (Or, if you have no children, how were you taught wisdom by your parents?)

_____

_____

7. What specific *principles* of money management would you like to teach your children?

FOUR PRINCIPLES OF MONEY MANAGEMENT

a. _____

_____

b. _____

_____

c. _____

_____

d. _____

_____

8. What specific *skills* of money management would you like to teach your children?

FOUR SKILLS OF MONEY MANAGEMENT

a. _____

_____

b. _____

_____

c. _____

_____

d. _____

_____

9. What are some creative ideas you have used or heard of for teaching children about handling money.

_____

_____

_____

_____

10. How do you think your children can make a difference in the next generation if you teach them how to handle their money according to God's principles?

_____

_____

_____

_____

11. What are some of the main things you've learned during this session which you are going to apply in your life?

_____

_____

_____

_____

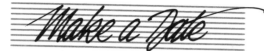

Make a date with your mate to meet in the next few days to complete **HomeBuilders Project #7.**

Date	Time	Location

■

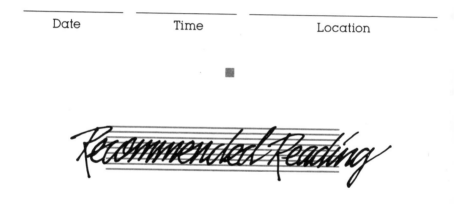

Raising Money-Smart Kids   by Ron and Judy Blue

■ A practical guide to help you teach your children how to handle money.

Individually—15–20 Minutes

1. List your greatest concerns regarding *how* you are training your children in money management and *what* you are teaching them.

_____

_____

_____

_____

2. List your greatest concerns about what you are teaching your children regarding their spiritual destiny.

_____

_____

_____

_____

Interact As a Couple—25–30 Minutes

1. Discuss your individual answers to the previous two questions.

2. List below the financial legacy that you would like to leave to your children.

_____

_____

3. List below some specific things you'd like to do in the next year to teach your children about finances.

_____

_____

_____

_____

4. Pull out your calendar and decide on some family and individual times when you can start implementing your plan.

One Final Project

Now that you've spent several weeks learning biblical concepts of handling money, the next step is to *put together a budget* and then *stick to it.*

1. Turn to your charts from **HomeBuilders Projects #3** and **#6.** Using these as a reference and asking God for guidance (see Session Four), decide what you should allocate to each area of expenditure listed on the next few pages.

2. Some key questions you'll need to ask yourself:

■ Are we saving enough for long-term needs?

■ Can we stay out of debt with this budget?

■ What do we have to sacrifice in order to stay with this budget? Are we willing to pay that price?

HOUSEHOLD BUDGET

(Date: _____)

MONTHLY INCOME: $_____

	MONTHLY	OTHER THAN MONTHLY	TOTAL
HOUSING			
Mortgage/rent	_____	_____	_____
Insurance	_____	_____	_____
Property taxes	_____	_____	_____
Electricity	_____	_____	_____
Heating	_____	_____	_____
Water	_____	_____	_____
Sanitation	_____	_____	_____
Telephone	_____	_____	_____
Cleaning	_____	_____	_____
Repairs/ Maintenance	_____	_____	_____
Supplies	_____	_____	_____
Other	_____	_____	_____
TOTAL	_____	_____	_____
FOOD	_____	_____	_____
CLOTHING	_____	_____	_____
TRANSPORTATION			
Insurance	_____	_____	_____
Gas and oil	_____	_____	_____
Maintenance/ Repairs	_____	_____	_____
Parking	_____	_____	_____
Other	_____	_____	_____
TOTAL	_____	_____	_____

	MONTHLY	OTHER THAN MONTHLY	TOTAL
ENTERTAINMENT/RECREATION			
Eating out			
Movies, concerts, etc.			
Baby-sitters			
Magazines/ Newspapers			
Vacation			
Clubs and activities			
Other			
TOTAL			
MEDICAL EXPENSES			
Insurance			
Doctors			
Dentists			
Medication			
TOTAL			
INSURANCE (OTHER THAN MEDICAL)			
Life			
Disability			
Other			
TOTAL			

	MONTHLY	OTHER THAN MONTHLY	TOTAL
CHILDREN			
School lunches			
Allowances			
Tuition			
Lessons			
Other			
TOTAL			
GIFTS			
Christmas			
Birthdays			
Anniversaries			
Other			
TOTAL			
MISCELLANEOUS			
Toiletries			
Husband misc.			
Wife misc.			
Cleaning, laundry			
Animal care			
Hair care			
Other			
Other			
TOTAL			
TOTAL LIVING EXPENSES			

Where Do You Go from Here?

As we learned in this study, finances and how you handle them play a big role in your marriage. Of the available options, either worldly or biblical, it's clear that the biblical guidelines God has ordained for us to use are indeed best. Often, the truths which Scripture unveils are simple, basic, and clear. This does not necessarily mean, however, that they are easy to implement on a practical day-to-day basis.

Building your marriage upon these truths may not be popular today, but it will have powerful results. You have probably already caught some special glimpses of that power through your investment of study, discussion, and application. If the truth within this couples study has at times shaken your marriage, it has done so only to strengthen it. We hope you have experienced a sense of strengthening.

But let's not stop here! If this HomeBuilders Couples Series study has helped you and your marriage, let's go on. And in going on, why not ask other couples to join you? By personally beginning another HomeBuilders study, you will not only add additional mortar to your own marriage; you will help strengthen other marriages as well. As Christians, we are not just trying to improve ourselves . . . we are trying to reach the world! This is our ultimate objective in The HomeBuilders Couples Series. Will you now help us help others?

Will you join us in touching lives and changing families?

The following are some practical ways you can make a difference in families today:

1. Gather a group of couples (four to seven) and lead them through the seven sessions of the HomeBuilders study you just completed.

2. Commit to participate in other HomeBuilders studies such as *Building Your Marriage, Building Your Mate's Self-Esteem,* or *Building Teamwork in Your Marriage.*

3. Begin weekly family nights—teaching your children about Christ, the Bible, and the Christian life.

4. Host an Evangelistic Dinner Party—invite your non-Christian friends to your home and as a couple share your faith in Christ and the forgiveness of His gospel.

5. Share the good news of Jesus Christ with neighborhood children.

6. If you have attended the FamilyLife Marriage Conference, why not assist your pastor in counseling premarrieds using the material you received?

7. If you are not a part of a growing church, join it and be baptized (if you haven't been baptized as a believer in Jesus Christ).

8. Show the film, *JESUS,* on video as an evangelistic outreach in you neighborhood. For more information, write to:

> Inspirational Media
> 30012 Ivy Glenn Dr., Suite 200
> Laguna Niguel, CA 92677

For more information on any of the above ministry opportunities, contact your local church, or write.

> FamilyLife
> P.O. Box 23840
> Little Rock, AR 72221-3840
> (501) 223-8663

133

The HomeBuilders

C O U P L E S   S E R I E S

"Unless the Lord builds the house,
they labor in vain who build it."
Psalm 127:1

The Four Spiritual Laws*

Just as there are physical laws that govern the physical universe, so are there spiritual laws which govern your relationship with God.

LAW ONE: God loves you and offers a wonderful plan for your life.

God's Love

"For God so loved the world, that He gave His only begotten Son, that whoever believes in Him should not perish, but have eternal life" (John 3:16).

God's Plan

(Christ speaking) "I came that they might have life, and might have it abundantly" (that it might be full and meaningful) (John 10:10).

Why is it that most people are not experiencing the abundant life? Because . . .

LAW TWO: Man is sinful and separated from God. Therefore, he cannot know and experience God's love and plan for his life.

Man Is Sinful

"For all have sinned and fall short of the glory of God" (Romans 3:23).

Man was created to have fellowship with God; but, because of his stubborn self-will, chose to go his own independent way, and fellowship with God was broken. This self-will, characterized by an attitude of active rebellion or passive indifference, is evidence of what the Bible calls sin.

Man Is Separated

"For the wages of sin is death" (spiritual separation from God) (Romans 6:23).

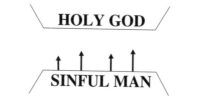

This diagram illustrates that God is holy and man is sinful. A great gulf separates the two. The arrows illustrate that man is continually trying to reach God and the abundant life through his own efforts, such as a good life, philosophy, or religion.

The third law explains the only way to bridge this gulf . . .

LAW THREE: Jesus Christ is God's only provision for man's sin. Through Him you can know and experience God's love and plan for your life.

He Died in Our Place

"But God demonstrates His own love toward us, in that while we were yet sinners, Christ died for us" (Romans 5:8).

He Rose from the Dead

"Christ died for our sins . . . He was buried . . . He was raised on the third day according to the Scriptures . . . He appeared to

[Peter], then to the twelve. After that He appeared to more than five hundred . . ." (1 Corinthians 15:3–6).

He Is the Only Way to God

"Jesus said to him, 'I am the way, and the truth, and the life; no one comes to the Father, but through Me'" (John 14:6).

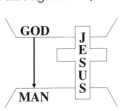

This diagram illustrates that God has bridged the gulf which separates us from Him by sending His Son, Jesus Christ, to die on the cross in our place to pay the penalty for our sins.

It is not enough just to know these three laws . . .

LAW FOUR: We must individually receive Jesus Christ as Savior and Lord; then we can know and experience God's love and plan for our lives.

We Must Receive Christ

"But as many as received Him, to them He gave the right to become children of God, even to those who believe in His name" (John 1:12).

We Receive Christ through Faith

"For by grace you have been saved through faith; and that not of yourselves, it is the gift of God; not as a result of works, that no one should boast" (Ephesians 2:8–9).

When We Receive Christ, We Experience a New Birth

(Read John 3:1–8.)

We Receive Christ by Personal Invitation

(Christ is speaking): "Behold, I stand at the door and knock; if any one hears My voice and opens the door, I will come in to him" (Revelation 3:20).

Receiving Christ involves turning to God from self (repentance) and trusting Christ to come into our lives to forgive our sins and to make us the kind of people He wants us to be. Just to agree intellectually that Jesus Christ is the Son of God and that He died on the cross for our sins is not enough. Nor is it enough to have an emotional experience. We receive Jesus Christ by faith, as an act of the will.

These two circles represent two kinds of lives:

SELF-DIRECTED LIFE

S—Self is on the throne
†—Christ is outside the life
•—Interests are directed by self, often resulting in discord and frustration

CHRIST-DIRECTED LIFE

†—Christ is in the life and on the throne
S—Self is yielding to Christ
•—Interests are directed by Christ, resulting in harmony with God's plan

Which circle best represents your life?

Which circle would you like to have represent your life?

You Can Receive Christ Right Now by Faith through Prayer

(Prayer is talking with God.)

God knows your heart and is not so concerned with your words as He is with the attitude of your heart. The following is a suggested prayer:

> "Lord Jesus, I need You. Thank You for dying on the cross for my sins. I open the door of my life and receive You as my Savior and Lord. Thank You for forgiving my sins and giving me eternal life. Make me the kind of person You want me to be."

Does this prayer express the desire of your heart?

If it does, pray this prayer right now, and Christ will come into your life, as He promised.

APPENDIX B

Have You Made the Wonderful Discovery of the Spirit-Filled Life?*

E very day can be an exciting adventure for the Christian who knows the reality of being filled with the Holy Spirit and who lives constantly, moment by moment, under His gracious control.

T he Bible tells us that there are three kinds of people:

1. NATURAL MAN (one who has not received Christ)

"But a natural man does not accept the things of the Spirit of God; for they are foolishness to him, and he cannot understand them, because they are spiritually appraised" (1 Corinthians 2:14).

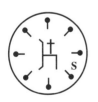

SELF-DIRECTED LIFE

S —Ego or finite self is on the throne
†—Christ is outside the life
•—Interests are controlled by self, often resulting in discord and frustration

2. SPIRITUAL MAN (one who is controlled and empowered by the Holy Spirit)

"But he who is spiritual appraises all things . . ." (1 Corinthians 2:15).

CHRIST-DIRECTED LIFE

†—Christ is on the throne of the life
S —Ego or self is dethroned
•—Interests are under control of infinite God, resulting in harmony with God's plan

3. CARNAL MAN (one who has received Christ, but who lives in defeat because he trusts in his own efforts to live the Christian life)

SELF-DIRECTED LIFE

E—Ego or finite self is on the throne
†—Christ is dethroned
● —Interests are controlled by self, often resulting in discord and frustration

"And I, brethren, could not speak to you as to spiritual men, but as to carnal men, as to babes in Christ. I gave you milk to drink, not solid food; for you were not yet able to receive it. Indeed, even now you are not yet able, for you are still carnal. For since there is jealousy and strife among you, are you not fleshly, and are you not walking like mere men?" (1 Corinthians 3:1–3).

A. God has Provided for Us an Abundant and Fruitful Christian Life.

Jesus said, "I came that they might have life, and might have it abundantly" (John 10:10).

"I am the vine, you are the branches; he who abides in Me, and I in him, he bears much fruit; for apart from Me you can do nothing" (John 15:5).

"But the fruit of the Spirit is love, joy, peace, patience, kindness, goodness, faithfulness, gentleness, self-control; against such things there is no law" (Galatians 5:22, 23).

"But you shall receive power when the Holy Spirit has come upon you; and you shall be My witnesses both in Jerusalem, and in all Judea and Samaria, and even to the remotest part of the earth" (Acts 1:8).

THE SPIRITUAL MAN

Some Personal Traits Which Result from Trusting God:

Christ-centered
Empowered by the Holy Spirit
Introduces others to Christ
Effective prayer life
Understands God's Word
Trusts God
Obeys God

Love
Joy
Peace
Patience
Kindness
Goodness
Faithfulness

The degree to which these traits are manifested in the life depends upon the extent to which the Christian trusts the Lord with every detail of his life, and upon his maturity in Christ. One who is only beginning to understand the ministry of the Holy Spirit should not be discouraged if he is not as fruitful as more mature Christians who have known and experienced this truth for a longer period.

Why is it that most Christians are not experiencing the abundant life?

B. Carnal Christians Cannot Experience the Abundant and Fruitful Christian Life.

The carnal man trusts in his own efforts to live the Christian life:

1. He is either uninformed about, or has forgotten, God's love, forgiveness, and power (Romans 5:8–10; Hebrews 10:1–25; 1 John 1; 2:1–3; 2 Peter 1:9; Acts 1:8).

2. He has an up-and-down spiritual experience.

3. He cannot understand himself—he wants to do what is right, but cannot.

4. He fails to draw upon the power of the Holy Spirit to live the Christian life.

(1 Corinthians 3:1–3; Romans 7:15–24; 8:7; Galatians 5:16–18)

THE CARNAL MAN

Some or all of the following traits may characterize the Christian who does not fully trust God:

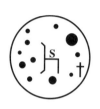

Ignorance of his
　spiritual heritage
Unbelief
Disobedience
Loss of love for God and
　for others
Poor prayer life
No desire for Bible study

Legalistic attitude
Discouragement
Impure thoughts
Jealousy
Guilt
Critical spirit
Worry
Frustration
Aimlessness

(The individual who professes to be a Christian but who continues to practice sin should realize that he may not be a Christian at all, according to 1 John 2:3; 3:6–9; Ephesians 5:5.)

The third truth gives us the only solution to this problem . . .

C. Jesus Promised the Abundant and Fruitful Life as the Result of Being Filled (Controlled and Empowered) by the Holy Spirit.

The Spirit-filled life is the Christ-controlled life, by which Christ lives His life in and through us in the power of the Holy Spirit (John 15).

1. One becomes a Christian through the ministry of the Holy Spirit, according to John 3:1–8. From the moment of spiritual birth, the Christian is indwelt by the Holy Spirit at all times (John 1:12; Colossians 2:9–10; John 14:16–17). Though all Christians are indwelt by the Holy Spirit, not all Christians are filled (controlled and empowered) by the Holy Spirit.

2. The Holy Spirit is the source of the overflowing life (John 7:37–39).

3. The Holy Spirit came to glorify Christ (John 16:1–5). When one is filled with the Holy Spirit, he is a true disciple of Christ.

4. In His last command before His ascension, Christ promised the power of the Holy Spirit to enable us to be witnesses for Him (Acts 1:1–9).

How, then, can one be filled with the Holy Spirit?

D. We Are Filled (Controlled and Empowered) by the Holy Spirit by Faith; Then We Can Experience the Abundant and Fruitful Life Which Christ Promised to Each Christian.

You can appropriate the filling of the Holy Spirit *right now* if you:

1. Sincerely desire to be controlled and empowered by the Holy Spirit (Matthew 5:6; John 7:37–39).

2. Confess your sins.

By faith thank God that He has forgiven all of your sins—past, present, and future—because Christ died for you (Colossians 2:13–15; 1 John 1; 2:1–3; Hebrews 10:1–17).

3. By faith claim the fullness of the Holy Spirit, according to:

a. HIS COMMAND—Be filled with the Spirit. "And do not get drunk with wine, for that is dissipation, but be filled with the Spirit" (Ephesians 5:18).

b. HIS PROMISE—He will always answer when we pray according to His will. "And this is the confidence which we have before Him, that, if we ask anything according to His will, He hears us. And if we know that He hears us in whatever we ask, we know that we have the requests which we have asked from Him" (1 John 5:14–15).

Faith can be expressed through prayer . . .

145

How to Pray in Faith to Be Filled with the Holy Spirit

We are filled with the Holy Spirit by *faith* alone. However, true prayer is one way of expressing your faith. The following is a suggested prayer:

> "Dear Father, I need You. I acknowledge that I have been in control of my life; and that, as a result, I have sinned against You. I thank You that You have forgiven my sins through Christ's death on the cross for me. I now invite Christ to again take control of the throne of my life. Fill me with the Holy Spirit as You commanded me to be filled, and as You promised in your Word that You would do if I asked in faith. I pray this in the name of Jesus. As an expression of my faith, I now thank You for taking control of my life and for filling me with the Holy Spirit."

Does this prayer express the desire of your heart? If so, bow in prayer and trust God to fill you with the Holy Spirit right now.

How to Know that You are Filled (Controlled and Empowered) by the Holy Spirit

Did you ask God to fill you with the Holy Spirit? Do you know that you are now filled with the Holy Spirit? On what authority? (On the trustworthiness of God Himself and His Word: Hebrews 11:6; Romans 14:22–23).

Do not depend upon feelings. The promise of God's Word, not our feelings, is our authority. The Christian lives by faith (trust) in the trustworthiness of God Himself and His Word. This train diagram illustrates the relationship between **fact** (God and His Word), **faith** (our trust in God and His Word), and **feeling** (the result of our faith and obedience) (John 14:21).

The train will run with or without the caboose. However, it would be futile to attempt to pull the train by the caboose. In the same way, we, as Christians, do not depend upon feelings or emotions, but we place our faith (trust) in the trustworthiness of God and the promises of His Word.

How to Walk in the Spirit

Faith (trust in God and His promises) is the only means by which a Christian can live the Spirit-controlled life. As you continue to trust Christ moment by moment:

1. Your life will demonstrate more and more of the fruit of the Spirit (Galatians 5:22–23); and will be more and more conformed to the image of Christ (Romans 12:2; 2 Corinthians 3:18).

2. Your prayer life and study of God's Word will become more meaningful.

3. You will experience His power in witnessing (Acts 1:8).

4. You will be prepared for spiritual conflict against the world (1 John 2:15–17); against the flesh (Galatians 5:16–17); and against Satan (1 Peter 5:7–9; Ephesians 6:10–13).

5. You will experience His power to resist temptation and sin (1 Corinthians 10:13; Philippians 4:13; Ephesians 1:19–23; 6:10; 2 Timothy 1:7; Romans 6;1–16).

Spiritual Breathing

By faith you can continue to experience God's love and forgiveness.

If you become aware of an area of your life (an attitude or an action) that is displeasing to the Lord, even though you are walking with Him and sincerely desiring to serve Him, simply thank God that

He has forgiven your sins—past, present and future—on the basis of Christ's death on the cross. Claim His love and forgiveness by faith and continue to have fellowship with Him.

If you retake the throne of your life through sin—a definite act of disobedience—breathe spiritually.

Spiritual Breathing (exhaling the impure and inhaling the pure) is an exercise in faith that enables you to continue to experience God's love and forgiveness.

1. EXHALE—confess your sin—agree with God concerning your sin and thank Him for His forgiveness of it, according to 1 John 1:9 and Hebrews 10:1–25. Confession involves repentance—a change in attitude and action.

2. INHALE—surrender the control of your life to Christ, and appropriate (receive) the fullness of the Holy Spirit by faith. Trust that He now controls and empowers you, according to the *command* of Ephesians 5:18 and the *promise* of 1 John 5:14–15.

Ron Blue, a Certified Public Accountant, is the best-selling author of *Master Your Money* (Thomas Nelson, 1986), *Raising Money-Smart Kids* (Thomas Nelson, 1988), and *The Debt Squeeze* (Focus on the Family, 1989). Ron is also featured in a six-part "Master Your Money" video curriculum that brings together biblical principles and sound financial concepts. He is a regular columnist for *Moody Monthly* and *Physician* magazines.

Ron and his wife, Judy, live in Atlanta with their five children: Cynthia, Denise, Karen, Tim, and Michael.

Renew Your Commitment.

Y ou've just finished an inspiring study from **The HomeBuilders Couples Series™.** No doubt you've learned a lot of things about your mate that will help the two of you grow closer together for years to come. You've also learned a lot about God's Word, and how much it means to study the Bible with other couples. But don't let it stop here—lay the next block in the foundation of your marriage by beginning another **HomeBuilders** couples study. It will help you keep your marriage as strong, as dynamic, as solid as the day you said "I do."

Your Mate Is a Gift from God.

Growing together as one begins by accepting your husband or wife as God's perfect provision for your needs —and trusting that He knows what your needs are even better than you do. Receive your mate with open arms, and you'll begin to draw closer together—in incredible, heartfelt new ways.

Building Your Marriage
By Dennis Rainey
Study Guide S411172
Leader's Guide AB026

Turn Conflict into Love and Understanding.

Every marriage has its share of conflict. But you can turn conflict into something positive. Once you get into the habit of being a blessing even when you've been insulted, you'll discover for yourself that the result—a stronger, more exciting marriage—is well worth the effort.

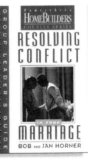

Resolving Conflict in Your Marriage
By Bob & Jan Horner
Study Guide S411202
Leader's Guide AB031

Celebrate and Enjoy Your Differences.

Once you understand that your differences are gifts from God, you'll see how they can help you enjoy each other more and make your relationship fun, healthy and fascinating. You are the unique person who is equipped to complete and fulfill your mate!

Building Teamwork in Your Marriage
By Robert Lewis
Study Guide S411181
Leader's Guide AB028

Marriage Is God's Workshop for Self-Esteem.

When you both know you are accepted, appreciated and free to risk failure, you'll experience new levels of love and fulfillment—personally and as a couple. It starts by putting past hurts behind you and bringing positive words to your mate that will strengthen, heal and encourage. This study will show you how.

Building Your Mate's Self-Esteem
By Dennis & Barbara Rainey
Study Guide S411199
Leader's Guide AB030

FAMILYLIFE

Look for these **HomeBuilders** couples studies at your local Christian bookstore.
Coming in June 1993: *Mastering Money in Your Marriage* and *Growing Together in Christ.*
Coming in Oct. 1993: *Managing Pressure in Your Marriage* and *Life Choices for a Lasting Marriage.*

Gospel Light

Four Ways to Keep Your Marriage Growing Strong.

Love Handles Everyone Will Want.

Every married person wants to hold on to romance. It's what keeps a marriage exciting. But often romance can slip away. *Holding on to Romance* explains how that special and elusive feeling can be recaptured. Norm Wright gives ideas of specific things to do and say that will rekindle the flame of passion in a marriage.

Holding on to Romance
By H. Norman Wright
Hardcover 5112168
ISBN 08307 15274

Communication Can Open Doors for Any Marriage.

Effective communication is the key to keeping a marriage healthy. Couples will immediately begin to improve their communication skills as they follow Norm Wright's steps toward coping with marital conflicts. This handbook also gives sound principles for building each other's self esteem and for handling angry feelings.

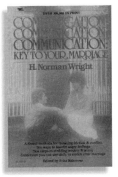

Communication:
Key to Your Marriage
By H. Norman Wright
Paperback 5415004
ISBN 08307 07263

What Makes a Man or a Woman Pleasing to God?

The Measure of a Man is an in-depth study of 20 characteristics that mark a mature Christian man. 1 and 2 Timothy and Titus.

The Measure of a Man
By Gene Getz
Paperback 5418472
ISBN 08307 10310

The Measure of a Woman is a practical, realistic study of 14 biblical ways a woman can be effective and fulfilled.

The Measure of a Woman
By Gene Getz
Paperback 5419940
ISBN 08307 13867

Ask for these books at your local Christian bookstore.

Gospel Light

"A Weekend to Remember"

Every couple has a unique set of needs. The FamilyLife Marriage Conference meets couples' needs by equipping them with proven solutions that address practically every component of "How to Build a Better Marriage." The conference gives you the opportunity to slow down and focus on your spouse and your relationship. You will spend an insightful weekend together, doing fun couples' projects and hearing from dynamic speakers on real-life solutions for building and enhancing oneness in your marriage.

You'll learn:

◆ *Five secrets of successful marriage*
◆ *How to implement oneness in your marriage*
◆ *How to maintain a vital sexual relationship*
◆ *How to handle conflict*
◆ *How to express forgiveness to one another*

Our insightful speaker teams also conduct sessions for:

◆ *Soon-to-be-marrieds*
◆ *Men-only*
◆ *Women-only*

The FamilyLife Marriage Conference

To register or receive a free brochure and schedule, call **FamilyLife at 1-800-333-1433**.

FAMILYLIFE

A ministry of Campus Crusade for Christ International

Take a Weekend...to Raise Your Children for a Lifetime

Good parents aren't just born that way; they begin with a strong, biblical foundation and then work at improving their parenting skills. That's where we come in.

In one weekend the FamilyLife Parenting Conference will equip you with the principles and tools you need to be more effective parents for a lifetime. Whether you're just getting started or in the turbulent years of adolescence, we'll show you the biblical blueprints for raising your children. You'll hear from dynamic speakers and do fun parenting skills projects designed to help you apply what you've learned. You'll receive proven, effective principles from parents just like you who have dedicated their lives to helping families.

You'll learn how to:

- ◆ *Build a strong relationship with your child*
- ◆ *Help your child develop emotional, spiritual and sexual identity*
- ◆ *Develop moral character in your child*
- ◆ *Give your child a sense of mission*
- ◆ *Pass on your values to your child*

The FamilyLife Parenting Conference
To register or receive a free brochure and schedule, call
FamilyLife at 1-800-333-1433.

FAMILYLIFE
A ministry of Campus Crusade for Christ International

FamilyLife Resources

Building Your Mate's Self-Esteem

The key to a joy-filled marriage is a strong sense of self-worth in both partners. This practical, best-selling book helps you tap into God's formula for building up your mate. How to overcome problems from the past, how to help your mate conquer self-doubt, how to boost communication, and much more. Creative "Esteem-Builder Projects" will bring immediate results, making your marriage all it can be. The #1 best-seller at FamilyLife Marriage Conferences across America.

Paperback, $8.95

Pulling Weeds, Planting Seeds

Thirty-eight insightful, thought-provoking chapters, laced with humor, show how you can apply the wisdom of God's Word to your life and home. Includes chapters on making your time with your family count, dealing with tough situations at home and at work, living a life of no regrets, and MUCH MORE. These bite-sized, fun-to-read chapters make this great book hard to put down.

Hardcover, $12.95

Staying Close

Overcome the isolation that creeps into so many marriages, and watch your marriage blossom! This best-selling book, winner of the 1990 Gold Medallion Award for best book on marriage and family, is packed with practical ideas and HomeBuilders projects to help you experience the oneness God designed for your marriage. How to manage stress. How to handle conflict. How to be a great lover. And much more! Based on 15 years of research and favorite content from the FamilyLife Marriage Conference.

Paperback, $10.95

The Questions Book

Discover the miracle of truly understanding each other. This book will lead you into deeper intimacy and joy by giving you 31 sets of fun, thought-provoking questions you can explore and answer together. Space is provided for you to write your answers. Share your innermost feelings, thoughts, goals, and dreams. This book could lead to the best times you'll ever spend together. **Hardcover, $9.95**

For more information on these and other FamilyLife Resources contact your local Christian retailer or call FamilyLife at 1-800-333-1433.

HomeBuilders Evaluation

Your First Name   Last Name

Spouse's First Name   Wedding Date   Your Age

Home Phone   Work Phone

Address

City   State   ZIP Code

Full Church Name   May we quote you? ☐ Yes ☐ No

Church City   State

How would you rate this HomeBuilders Couples study?

                       Poor   Excellent

Overall experience   1   2   3   4   5   6   7   8   9   10

Study Guide   1   2   3   4   5   6   7   8   9   10

How many HomeBuilders Couples Series have you now participated in ? [ ]
Describe the effect this HomeBuilders study has had on you and your family:

How would you change or improve this HomeBuilders study?

Would you be willing to lead a separate HomeBuilders study yourself?
☐ Yes   ☐ No   ☐ Yes, with more training

Have you attended a FamilyLife Conference? ☐ Yes ☐ No

FamilyLife has many other resources for you and your family. Please check if you would like to receive additional information on the following resources:

☐ Other HomeBuilders Couples Series studies
☐ FamilyLife Marriage Conference
☐ FamilyLife Parenting Conference
☐ "FamilyLife Today" radio program
☐ Books, videos and tapes

BUSINESS REPLY MAIL

FIRST-CLASS MAIL   PERMIT NO.4092   LITTLE ROCK, AR

POSTAGE WILL BE PAID BY ADDRESSEE

FAMILY LIFE
P O BOX 23840
LITTLE ROCK AR 72221-9940